THE IMPOSSIBLE DREAM

THE SPIRITUALITY OF DOM HELDER CAMARA

The Impossible Dream
The Spirituality of Dom Helder Camara

by

MARY HALL

ORBIS BOOKS
Maryknoll, New York 10545

The Catholic Foreign Mission Society of America (Maryknoll) recruits and trains people for overseas missionary service. Through Orbis Books Maryknoll aims to foster the international dialogue that is essential to mission. The books published, however, reflect the opinions of their authors and are not meant to represent the official position of the society.

Library of Congress Cataloging in Publication Data

Hall, Mary, Ph.D.
   The impossible dream.

   Includes bibliographical references.
   1. Câmara, Hélder, 1909-   2. Catholic Church—
Bishops—Biography.   3. Bishops—Brazil—Biography.
I. Title.
BX4705.C2625H34   1980   282'.092'4 [B]   79-26888
ISBN 0-88344-212-4 pbk.

First published by Christian Journals Limited, 2 Bristow Park, Upper Malone Road, Belfast BT96TH, Northern Ireland, and 760 Somerset Street W, Ottawa, Ontario, Canada

Copyright © Christian Journals Limited 1979

U.S. Edition 1980 by Orbis Books, Maryknoll, New York 10545

Typeset in Ireland and printed and bound in the United States of America

Contents

FOR THOMAS McCREADY, Engineer, O.B.E.

Foreword

For Dom Helder Camara, Catholic Archbishop of Olinda and Recife in North-East Brazil, to 'dream the impossible dream' but even more to strive for the impossible goal is necessary to the human soul which would rise above drabness and bondage. He, too, wants to ride forth through the world righting wrongs, defending the helpless, attempting to establish an ideal system of justice. Like Don Quixote, like Christ himself, he is a reformer wishing to establish the knight errant's 'Golden Age', the kingdom of God on earth. In his wanderings Don Quixote meets innkeepers, noblemen, peasant girls and duchesses, criminals, actors, students, judges and priests; all types, good and bad, high and low, forming a complete portrait gallery of contemporary Spain. To the few rooms in Manguinhos—the former Episcopal Palace—that Dom Helder uses as offices come crowds of anonymous poor, students, priests, journalists, government officials, the representative face of Brazil. He speaks to all he meets with the simplicity of a child, yet it is obvious that his words give politicians sleepless nights.

Both Dom Helder and Don Quixote have messianic qualities. Their message is pure. It is enobling. It speaks to the heart in Brazil as in Spain. The ignorant man of goodwill, whether it be Sancho Panza or Severino, understands him. The depised victims of man's brutality, whether it be Aldonza or Magdalena, understand him. But the representatives of the established order, Sanson the Padre, or the Brazilian Government, do not understand. Dom Helder himself once remarked:

"I'm very fond of Don Quixote. He is much more realistic than is generally believed. When I face a crowd of people as I did tonight, I have the impression that my talk about overthrowing structures without armed force is, for a number of the young,

7

quixotic. And yet there is realism in it, I might say political realism . . . . " [1]

"If the African slaves in Brazil were emancipated thanks to the enthusiasm of Castro Alves, Ruy Barbosa, Joaquim Nabuco, why cannot we, all united, succeed in peacefully overthrowing the old structures and laying down new foundations?" [2]

In his strong belief in mankind Dom Helder sees himself as a Don Quixote, and perhaps this comparison best illustrates what kind of person he is. When against the Goliath of injustice on a world scale he enters the lists armed with his faith and confidence he endorses his own words, that "only the ingenuous and those without creative imagination still think that Quixotism means idealism without practical consequences". His passion for the possible—and for the impossible—makes him refuse to rest content with the "scandal of sub-men stuck in a subhuman life, trapped by subhuman work". In the preface to his book *Race Against Time* he writes: "Here is everything I prize, always dreaming, always hoping, striving every day to love more".

It is to the 'Abrahamic minorities', as he names them, in his own country and throughout the world that Dom Helder calls, to get moving towards making their own environment more just and human. Abraham—of the Jews, the Christians, the Muslims —was the first to be called by God to set out, face hardship, arouse his brothers and encourage them to start moving. Dom Helder believes in the fact that all over the world, among all races, languages, religions, ideologies, there are men and women ready to serve their neighbour, ready for any sacrifice for the good of men, ready to build a more just and more human world.

In Maurice West's novel, *The Shoes of the Fisherman,* Pope Cyril says: "I hope and pray for a great movement, a great man, who will shake us and bring us back to life, for example a man like Francis of Assisi. What does he stand for? For a complete break with the pattern of history, a sudden and inexplicable renewal of the primitive Christian spirit".

As Dom Helder Camara the Don Quixote of Brazil rides forth against the impregnable walls of unjust old structures that must be overthrown, may not the troubadour of the hills and valleys of Italy have returned in our century as the troubadour of the sierras of Brazil? The terrain is different, but the song and the needs are the same—the love of Christ for the poor and lowly of the earth—to which everything bears witness from Brother Sun to the ant and the rose-bush.

This book is written to share the memories of the days I spent with Dom Helder in Recife in search of a bishop's soul. My thanks firstly to him who gave so generously of his own time and without whom the tapes and their translation in book form would not have been possible.

My thanks also to his friends of many years Cecelia Monteiro and Marina Bandeira for their valued time and hospitality.

1

Arrived

The noise in Rio de Janeiro's crowded airport terminal is overwhelming, and so is the heat. My effort at communicating in French with the desk clerk fails and my companion Cecelia Monteiro—Dom Helder's secretary of many years—takes over the negotiation of baggage. I relinquish the responsibility gratefully and stand aside in the din hardly believing I am on the last lap of a journey that has taken me via London, Madrid, New York, Washington, Miami, Lima and Rio.

"We deserve a cold drink", Cecelia says as she hands me my boarding pass for Recife, Northeast Brazil. There is no place to sit so we perambulate as best we can between the jostling groups and ever watchful soldiers. Children dart between us, adults shoulder us apart and conversation is fitful, fragments of advice, repetition of messages, reminders about letters, questions. The flight to Recife is called. A warm abraço for Cecelia.

"Thank you for everything, your hospitality, your help and sharing. I will always remember the hours we have spent together. Good-bye! Good-bye!" The diminutive figure is lost to sight. A short walk across the fiery tarmac to the Varig plane. As we are airborne the collage of my weeks in Rio unfolds. Friends, contacts, buildings, taxi rides, sun and sand and samba music, interviews in condominiums and favelas, hours and days of colours, of talking and absorbing against the backdrop of Rio's incredibly beautiful island-dotted bay. Interviews! The thought strikes of all those tapes in my luggage. What if the baggage is mislaid? I had been warned to guard them carefully and had chosen to wrap them in clothing and pack them rather than carry them and risk inspection of hand-luggage. I remind myself that they are anonymous as all had requested me to omit their names and location. But a few weeks in Rio has taught me to respect those fears and an uneasiness tugs at me for the rest of the journey.

Recife airport is a repeat version of the concrete design I have seen so often before. A short walk to the small group of people awaiting passengers, and oh! the relief after weeks of Portuguese and French an Irish brogue calling my name. The voice belongs to an immediately recognizable Irish face.

"Paddy Leonard, Holy Ghost Father".

"This is Senorina Lila Wallach—Dom Helder sent us to meet you".

I discover I have a choice of residence in Recife, the Holy Ghost Fathers' mission house in Paroquia N.S. dos Remedios, Madalena, or Senorina Wallach's home. I opt for the former as it is nearer Dom Helder's house.

"Which is your luggage?"

"I can't see it!"

Paddy goes to investigate. While he is away Lila explains that Dom Helder used to meet visitors himself but it attracts so much attention for his guests from the authorities that he now sends emissaries. Paddy returns carrying one case.

"I'm afraid your other case hasn't arrived".

"Oh! No! It has my tapes in it!"

I explain my distress.

"Don't worry. They have promised to get it by nightfall".

I do worry.

On the drive through Recife exchange of curricula vitae takes precedence over attention to the route. After some time I notice we are driving along a wide dusty road of scattered houses and stores, and Lila stops the car at a wide verge on the left fronting a cemented unfinished two-storied building set well back from the road. A factory? A store? I'm not sure. We say goodbye to Lila and promise to visit her in a few days. Paddy and I cross the uneven ground typical of a building site. We circle the building on the right hand side and I discover it has no gable wall beyond the ground floor. It is flanked at a distance by an overgrown tidal stream of Recife's big port. We enter a long cemented passageway of half walls with big rooms on either side, and at the end a door leads into a living room cum study, with books spilling on to most of the furniture. The doorway of the adjoining kitchenette is filled by the tall figure of Fr. Frank Murphy, parish priest.

"Welcome to Madalena!"

He takes me to my room which he vacated for me, I discover

later. I also discover that the only shower in the house is part of my suite, that there are no other rooms downstairs, that a cement staircase leads from the kitchenette to the small chapel upstairs as well as several unfinished rooms equipped only with hammocks.

"Dom Helder will see you at 12 to-morrow", Frank informs me at tea-time. Before I can answer, the door opens and a bearded teen-ager carrying a guitar comes in and joins us. He is the first of many I am to meet who use a house where they know there is always a welcome, food and a hammock. From them I am to learn about young Brazil.

Galway man Frank Murphy lectures in English at the University of Recife. His salary is used to augment the meagre financial situation of his pastoral flock on the fringes of Recife's large port. This human flotsam and jetsam is indeed deprived, and Frank—for most of his life an educator—has gathered the children of the area together for classes. School is conducted by teachers working both shifts of a two-shift day in the large rooms on the ground floor of the building. Their salary, for working in these crowded classrooms with a minimum of facilities and a maximum of noise from class rote learning, less than a pittance by European standards.

"Our water supply is very erratic", Frank warns me as I prepare to retire. How true! After a long day I decide to take a shower and having worked up a good lather of shampoo on my hair the water jet suddenly diminishes to a mere trickle and then to drops. I recount the emergency situation through the closed door to Frank and Paddy who are still chatting in the living room. After many instructions, the noise of much cranking of machinery in the distance and a long wait the water re-appears.

Later, I creep under my mosquito net to dream of newspaper headlines: 'Tapes seized, collaborators arrested!'' I awake with relief to the church bell tolling overhead and sunlight streaming into the room.

2

First meeting

Next morning Paddy and I set out for our appointment with Dom Helder. We leave in good time as I have decided to try and call Marina Bandeira in Rio about my lost luggage, before meeting with Dom Helder. Salt breezes and sunshine as we walk the streets lined with waving coconut trees. Crossing the road between non-stop VW's is a major hazard. Brazilian drivers seem to forget their cars have brakes. We cross a bridge.

"Dom Helder's church is at the end of this road on the left. There! his house is behind the wall".

Paddy points to a lower wall continuing from the wall of the church, in which is set a wooden door. The house itself is not visible.

"He wanted to rent the house next door, but the rent was too high, the equivalent of about £12 a month. So he had the sacristy of the church partitioned into three rooms".

I notice the wall is pitted with holes—the marks of bullets— and daubed with slogans. Pat translates one as 'Go home, communist Archbishop'.

We pass Ingreja das Fronteiras, on to the Convent of the Sisters of Charity where Pat explains my luggage problems to the portress and we are escorted to the convent phone. After many trials and errors Marina's voice answers. I had been warned about tapped phones so I can't be too explicit, but Marina senses the cause of my anxiety and promises that she will go herself to the airport and trace the missing bag. Her reassurance comforts me greatly and I leave for my meeting with Dom Helder with a lightened heart. We walk a short distance to a rambling old house set back from the road. It is the venue, Pat explains, for a group of women who are having a day of prayer and recollection. Dom Helder is addressing them this morning.

We traverse a rather overgrown path turning right towards the front door, pausing for a moment on hearing a man's voice.

"Dom Helder", Paddy nods in recognition as we open the door. Rows of empty chairs against the wall greet our view, but at the opposite end of the room is a group of 20-25 seated women. Standing facing them is a slight figure about 5'3" in a loose fitting black soutane and clerical collar. A large chain with a simple wooden cross hangs about his neck. Changing expressions flit across his mobile face, rising and falling inflections of voice match up with gesticulating arms. I stand absorbed until I notice Paddy has sat down and is writing in a notebook. I join him, still watching Dom Helder who is now speaking in a hushed voice with closed eyes until he finally relapses into silence. No one stirs. A white butterfly rides in on the sunlight streaming through a window near Dom Helder. His faded cassock lightens to grey. He opens his eyes and his arms embrace all present and says a few words, then begins to read from a paper he picks up from the table in front of him. Paddy begins to write again. Dom Helder is moving about, glancing from the paper to search now one face of his audience, now another. He nods, emphasises a point with a gesture and is silent once again. Paddy passes me his notebook. One column of the page is written in Portuguese. 'Rough translation' heads the opposite column, and I read:

Strange Mystery

If you are amazed to see
that the divine plan hung on the lips of Mary
what will you say when you see
that year after year
at your front door
God himself awaits
for your Yes?

I have had my introduction to Dom Helder's soul.

After the meeting, Dom Helder is surrounded by his friends, and Paddy and I walk out in the garden.

"Does he write a lot of poetry?"

"Yes! Every night after some sleep he gets up and writes his meditations in this way. His friends make collections of his poems. He always signs them with his pen-name—Don José".

I am about to ask why when Dom Helder joins us. At close

range it is his eyes that I notice, startlingly penetrating and trusting. His face is deeply lined. He greets each of us with a warm abraco. This is the typical Brazilian greeting of enfolding arms, cheeks pressed to each other on either side with kisses blown to the air. I notice how much smaller he is than my 5'11" and as I stoop to embrace him, his frame seems as frail as a bird's.

"Come and have lunch with us and we can talk".

We cross the garden and enter a courtyard which leads into a large room dwarfed by a trestle-table laden with food. The chairs are already occupied by the retreatants and Dom Helder goes to the head of the table and gestures to the two places vacant for us on his left and right. He says grace, followed by a few words introducing us to the group, and sits down. The women break into an excited chatter. Two of them bring large dishes of meat to the table. Dom Helder takes a token helping and some salad.

"Dom Helder, would you like me to speak in French or in English?"

"Ah! You speak French!"

"Yes! But with an Irish accent".

His face lights up.

"Then I will be happy to speak with you in French with a Brazilian accent. It is better than my English!"

He pats my hand and smiles that incredibly trusting smile of his I was to see so often and in so many circumstances.

"We should manage very well together".

After lunch we sit at the by-now-deserted table and talk.

"Tell me in one sentence why you have come to Recife?"

I answer, hesitating a little.

"I want to try and understand you, Dom Helder . . . . Why you are the kind of bishop you are".

"If you want to understand me you must come and live with me. Come! let us go to my little house".

We walk the short distance to his home down the road, past the Convent and the church to the little door in the wall. Dom Helder unlocks it and we follow him through a tiny garden 12' × 10' and along a path into a simple partitioned whitewashed room. Dom Helder seats us on two of the four chairs around a table in the right hand corner, opens the shutter and the window and leaves us to go into an adjoining room. A hammock across the window facing us is the only other furnishing, apart from a picture hanging on each wall. I study them. On my left a print

17

in black and white of an Andean shepherd boy playing a flute against a background of high mountains . . . . On one side of the window a painting of a cane field and against the tall crowded stalks the figure of a crucified labourer in working clothes and brimmed hat. In the background refinery buildings belching smoke into the sky . . . . To the left of the window is a painting of an angled street of high walls. Against one of them stands an unsmiling wide-eyed little girl clutching a doll. In the narrow space where the two walls converge is a glimpse of blue sky and deeper blue sea . . . . Above the table on my right is a straw image of the Virgin, obviously Mexican . . . .

Dom Helder returns with a big book and a pencil. "My diary" he says and sits at the table beside me. He turns the pages to to-day's date.

"To understand me you must be with me. Let us see. Here I am free, here I must go to the Chancellery. You can come with me. Here, yes! here yes! Yes. Yes".

He punctuates his phrases by drawing lines across the spaces in the diary. I have seldom seen time disposed of with such prodigality.

"The centre of each day is Mass at 6 a.m. Will you join me?"

I readily agree.

Before we leave I ask:

"Dom Helder, why did you choose these particular pictures?"

His face lights up as he points to the Andean shepherd.

"This shepherd boy has nothing but his flute, his song, and the gifts of mountain and air. I like to think of myself as a shepherd for my people. I too have a song, a song of God's love for each one".

He moves to the painting of the sugar cane.

"A Dutch artist painted this for me and it is so true. Many Nordestino's are crucified day after day by overwork, hunger, fatigue. You see the profits of the cane rising to the sky . . . but only the landowner gets richer".

A sadness on his face as he turns to the painting of the solemn-eyed little girl.

"Like so many of my children in the Northeast she has nothing but the sky and the sea".

And pointing to the Madonna.

"My mother, who always listens to me and answers my prayers".

He motions us into the other section of the partitioned sacristy which serves as a study; a simple desk, shelves lined with books, a chair, and a screen in the corner. Then into the adjacent room, an alcove really, with a skylight in the roof where the light shines on a simple flat bed. On the other side of the wall is the sanctuary of the church and the tabernacle. He smiles at us and points,

"I am never alone".

Helder Pessoa Camara was born on February 7, 1909, in Fortaleza, capital of the State of Ceara, Northeast Brazil.

His father, Joao Camara Filho, a book-keeper with the French importing firm Boris et Freres and part-time journalist, was a masonic freethinker. In spite of his being a Mason, his son's baptism in the local Catholic church was a matter of course, but the religious education of his children he left to their mother. Dona Adelaide Pessoa Camara would have liked to call her son José but Joao preferred Helder, a Dutch word meaning "fortress" which he came across in an encyclopedia. His mother was a grade school teacher who went to church only once a year. Helder was born and reared in a rented school-house. He was her twelfth child, born in the thirteenth year of her marriage. Six of her children died in early childhood, five of them of croup during a one-month period while she waited, helpless, for the remedy to reach Fortaleza.

3

A man with a song

Exactly at 6 a.m. Dom Helder comes out of the sacristy to the altar. The sanctuary is lit by the early morning sunlight and it lights Dom Helder's domed forehead as he arranges the chalice on the altar. Pat and I slip between the heavy wooden pews and kneel behind a small group of worshippers, mostly women. An early truck accelerates noisily on the street outside.

Dom Helder raises his head, opens his arms wide and high as if to encircle us all.

"In nome del Padre y del Filio y del Espiritu Santo".

"Oremos . . . . "

The ancient ritual proceeds, prayers and readings inflected and emphasized, gestures including the group of people present. As I approach the altar for Communion I notice Dom Helder looks directly at each one of us as he holds up the host.

"El corpo de nostro Senhor".

"Amen".

I return to my place.

"Amen for these days in Recife, for the opportunity to spend them with a man of God, a man of justice, a man with a song in his heart of God's care for his people".

After Mass I join Dom Helder in the sacristy and we go through to his little house for breakfast. The Sisters from the Convent have left our breakfast ready.

He explains the arrangement.

"They prepare one dish for me in the evening also. Lunch, I eat out with friends or at the Sisters' school".

The aroma of Brazilian coffee as well as anticipation of the day ahead gives me an appetite. The rolls and marmalade taste delicious. I notice—and was to note on many subsequent occasions—that conversation takes precedence over Dom

Helder's attention to food. Small helpings eaten as an accompaniment to exchange of views but he never wastes anything.

"Well! Let us begin", Dom Helder says as he clears the table. I set up the tape recorder.

The air is heavy with some pleasant but unrecognized scents from the Convent garden. The string hammock slung across the open window stirs slightly as a welcome gust of wind bends the coconut trees outside and enters the small white-washed room. Its movement shatters the geometric pattern of sunlight shining through the hammock's woven cords.

We sit at the small table in the corner. Despite the heat Dom Helder wears his black cassock, alert and bright-eyed as if for some noteworthy event. I smile across the table and he gestures towards my tape recorder. I press the dual switches.

"Can we begin at the beginning, Dom Helder?"

After a small pause he begins with downcast eyes looking at his open hands.

"I believe I owe a great deal to my father and to my mother. My mother—an exceptional woman, one of the greatest influences of my life—often called me José when she was pleased with me. She was not a person of wide culture: she was a grade school teacher. But since she was a kind person, her openness has marked the whole of my life. She had a great gift of human understanding, understanding for human weakness. 'José', she used often to say, 'whenever a person seems to us to be bad, if one gets near to him, if one makes the effort to know him from within, one discovers that the root cause is weakness. That is why Christ on Calvary said of those who had done more than the rest, who had left him naked, who had struck and wounded him, even of these, Forgive them, Father, they know not what they do . . . .'."

"She was rather strict with me. She used to say: You must give a good example. She was very demanding. One day, she expected even more than I could give. I started to cry. She led me from the classroom into our home. I thought that, for the first time, I would perhaps be slapped. Neither my father nor my mother had ever slapped me. But when we were all alone, she said to me: 'Son, forgive me. I demanded more than you could give'. Yes, she asked my pardon because she was sure she had made a mistake. That's very important, isn't it? To admit one's mistakes?" . . . . And here he chuckles and nods at me.

"My mother left a profound mark on my life as a man and as

22

a priest. One day my native town, Fortaleza, was shocked by the murder of a poet dearly loved by all. The whole town was thinking of his mother, crushed by her loss. My mother's comment was 'I don't know who I pity most—the mother of the murdered man or the mother of the assassin'. Such lessons of human sensibility she gave as a matter of course: by her example, her life . . . .

"It is to her that I owe my inability to eat alone the bread I can share with my neighbour, my brother. With her I saw all things with ever-new eyes, thus seeing things always for the very first time, dreading to humiliate anyone or see anyone humiliated. She taught me to see Jesus Christ in the person of the poor; to keep young in spirit . . . .

"She was my first teacher in a classroom that was part of the rented house in which I was born. Salaries of primary teachers and clerks were very low and were paid irregularly . . . .

"Many people ask me why and when I began to be interested in social justice. I could answer that this is the duty of any priest. But I cannot help but remember that I myself knew hunger and misery; that I saw my mother weep and my father fall silent from bitterness when there was nothing to eat, when there was not enough to break bread among their children. I didn't like okra. Once, I stopped eating when there was only okra on the plate. Next day my mother presented me with the same plate and said with a smile: 'Helder, this business of liking and not liking is a luxury only the rich can enjoy. Eat a little and you will see that it is good'. Since that day, I eat anything. I still don't like okra, but I always eat it, almost with enjoyment . . . . I only wish I had taken full advantage of all the lessons she taught me . . . . " He pauses as if remembering, and then continues:

"My grandfather had been the owner and editor of a newspaper. My father was a journalist also and had begun to write for the newspaper when it passed to another owner. He lost his job, but he continued to do freelance work, mostly theatre criticism. He had a keen interest in the arts. As a boy I was always at hand for rehearsals and performances of plays written by my uncle who was also my godfather. I have always loved the theatre . . . .

"I think my call to be a priest came only from God. There were no priests in our family, no pressures from clergy. When I was eight years old I told my father I wished to be a priest. He said, 'Do you know what it means to be a priest? It means to belong to yourself no more. The priest belongs to God and to others'. If I were not already convinced, this description would have convinced me. Carried away by what he had said, I exclaimed: 'But that is exactly what I want to be'. My father gave me his blessing and never interfered with my priestly vocation. Later we spent many years together in Rio. We always respected each other's convictions. He recovered his faith in God and the Church as an old man without my persuasion. I learnt from him to always respect the religious views of others''.

Dom Helder entered the Seminary of Sao José at Fortaleza on September 2, 1923. The local branch of the St. Vincent de Paul Society agreed to pay half his board and tuition fees.

"The main interests and preoccupations of the universal and Brazilian church, and so of those charged with the training of priests in the 20's, were communism, religious indifference, religious ignorance, lack of integration between religion and life, lack of church influence in public life. The alternative proposed included better religious education, formation of an intellectual elite, work with the masses through Catholic Action, greater participation by Catholics in the political life of the nation".[3] . . . Dom Helder's training also included the discovery of his talents and defects much to his own cost. The Seminary was staffed by Dutch Lazarists, members of the Congregation founded in 1625 by St. Vincent de Paul.

4

The birth of change

It takes us half an hour to walk to Rua Enrique Diaz and Dom Helder's house. At 3 p.m. we arrive at the little wooden door in the wall. To-day I am escorted on either side by two stalwart Holy Ghost Fathers. The guards on the opposite side of the road evince some interest and put their heads together. Dom Helder is amused as he opens the door.

"Imagine three visitors all the way from Ireland to see one old man".

We follow him along the tiny garden path and into the house. After introductions and some questions we sit around the table, Dom Helder and I with the tape recorder between us, facing John and Paddy. As John had previously been Dean of Studies in a Dublin Seminary, I begin by asking Dom Helder to tell us about his Seminary days.

"After learning all my mother could teach me, I was sent to a private teacher, Dona Salome Cisne, who prepared me for my entrance to the Seminary. Thanks to her I could almost have gone directly to philosophy, were it not for Latin. The most important lesson she taught me was that in spite of diplomas, we must never forget that we never stop being pupils . . . . My director in the Junior Seminary, Padre Cabral, was also my professor of philosophy and dogmatic theology. He taught us not only Trinitarian theories but how to live them. 'This week will be the week of the Father. In all you do remember the Father, that he is with you, that he has made all things, the sky and the light—everything for your benefit to share with others!' . . . . Next the week of the Son. 'Every time you meet someone, man, woman or child, remember that this is someone for whom Christ shed his blood and gave his life. In our prayer to the Holy Spirit: "Come, Holy Spirit, to enlighten and console" remember that the Spirit is already here because of Christ and it is not for us to bid him come, we must go to him.' . . . .

Cabral also gave me a vision of love so elevated and so positive that my head never filled with fantasies. I never was afraid of women. I never was afraid to love everything created. He used to say: 'The one who made man, from head to foot, was God. So there are no 'immoral' organs. It is the use we make of our organs that may be immoral.' . . . .

I was also greatly influenced by my French rector, a man of wide interests. He encouraged me to read widely in French and appointed me librarian, and I had to 'censor' the many books he received from publishers in France. One day he gave me a book with some pages clipped together. I refused it unless I could read it all and discuss my impressions with him later. He agreed . . . .

A friend and I who shared class prizes persuaded the rector to allow the class to study as a group. This gave me a chance to transmit what I knew to the others, an art that has helped me over the years . . . .

In the minor seminary one of the rules forbade the hundred or so students to speak in the corridors. I and many of my companions transgressed, and for this we were denied membership of a certain confraternity. Later at the major seminary when I was accepted for the tonsure, I requested that my companions and I be admitted also to the confraternity. I felt it was important to break up an old routine. This was an anomaly! an illogicality! a seminarian judged worthy of the tonsure by the Church while not eligible, for something of no importance, to be a member of a confraternity. The request was granted . . . .

On another occasion my personal locker was searched and some poems I had written discovered by the rector. He requested me to refrain from writing poetry until after my ordination and, great as the sacrifice was, I agreed. I knew my rector as a sincere man. I respected him as someone who discussed matters with his students and admitted when he was in the wrong. I didn't find the discipline in the Seminary easy but the years of training were happy and fruitful ones. To the Seminary I owe much of what I am".

The tape clicks to an end.

"Dom Helder, wouldn't you like a rest?"

His eyes sparkle.

28

"A good idea!"

He rises quickly and scurries into the tiny room next door. My two companions are silent with many thoughts. I, too, readjust the recorder in silence.

The years that Helder Camara spent in the Seminary (1923-31) were years of renewal for the Brazilian Church. The then Archbishop of Rio, Dom Sebastiao Leme, was the most enlightened Churchman of the period. Under his patronage the Centro Dom Vital was established in Rio as a centre, both social and educational, for Catholic intellectuals to counteract the 150 year old tradition of rationalism and anti-clericalism among Brazilian intellectuals. The review 'A Ordem' became the official organ of renewal and a platform for Catholic thought of the day. A young man from Sergipe in the Northeast, a recent convert, Jackson de Figueiredo, became director of the Centre and editor of 'A Ordem'.

5.

To the Seminary

Almost immediately Dom Helder returns clutching in his embrace two bottles, four glasses and a tin of biscuits. He bends and lowers them in a heap onto the table. Like a mischievous child he points to the bottle, the one in the wicker container and says with an infectious smile, "Let us have a celebration".
He fills my glass, and as he serves the others I remember other Episcopal teas on other shores. Silver salvers served by turbaned servants in white starched kurthas under whirling fans; dainty blue china in Italian palazzios behind shuttered windows; this one reminds me of home. Dom Helder fills his own glass from the water bottle. As the glasses of the others empty he refills them. I refuse.
"Non, non, Dom Helder! C'est assez! Ou je vais chanter!"
He insists.
"Ah! Mais oui! Buvez! Buvez! J'aimerais bien vous entendre chanter!"
Everyone laughs.
We continue to relax and chat. Dom Helder gathers up the glasses and we settle down once again to listen. Dom Helder begins with an exact repetition of his last sentence.
"Yes, to the Seminary I owe much of what I am . . . . Of course, I have always been interested in journalism because of my grandfather and my father, and while in the Seminary I began to write for the local Catholic daily 'O Nordeste'. One day I came across the class notes of a pupil at the Teacher Training College at Fortaleza, and I came to the conclusion that the psychology professor was teaching behaviourism. I showed the notes to the rector. 'We must reply', I said. 'We must help these students'.
"The rector and Seminary professors agreed and I sent an article to *O Nordeste,* under the pen-name Alceu da Silveira.

The article appeared in *O Nordeste* on July 23, 25 and 26 of 1930. The professor's replies appeared in the rival *O Povo* on July 24 and 28.

"The Vicar General of the Archdiocese, Msgr. Tabosa Braga, lived at the Seminary. He sent for me. I was absolutely certain that he wanted to commend me, to tell me how happy he was to read my articles. He asked, 'Is it true that these articles are really yours?' 'Yes, Father, it is true . . . . ' 'Then, my son, I must inform you that yesterday's article is your last'. 'But, Father! Excuse me, but have you read the terrible things that woman published in today's paper? Please, Father! At least the last article, tomorrow: I have already prepared it, I can show it to you . . . . ' 'Yesterday', he replied, 'you wrote your last article'.

"I left the room. The only explanation I could see for the attitude of the Vicar General was the fact that the professor, Dona Edith Braga, was his sister-in-law . . . .

"I went to the college chapel, and I am convinced that had I not managed to submit to the humiliation which had been sent me that day, I would have abandoned the Seminary and maybe the faith.

"I stayed in the chapel repeating, 'Holy Mother, I will not leave this place until I have recovered my calm'. I remembered that it was the feast-day of Saint Martha: July 29, and the words, 'Martha, Martha, you worry and fret about so many things and yet few are needed, indeed only one. It is Mary who has chosen the better part'. My defence of truth was revealed to me as pride, pride in my journalism and my own importance. I said a prayer of thanksgiving and left the chapel. When I rejoined my fellow students they urged me to continue the fight. 'Please', I begged them, 'Help me to understand that it was pride . . . . '

"On the following day, an announcement from Msgr. Braga on the first page of *O Nordeste* declared that the controversy was closed. Dona Edith had assured him that she had no intention of teaching heresy, that her references to ideas contrary to religion had never gone beyond the needs of the course. He had 'reached an understanding' with Alceu da Silveira who had promised to end the discussion!

"It was the first great humiliation of my life. God sends us four or five small humiliations each day and four or five big, first-class humiliations during our life-time . . . .

"Humility is indeed an essential virtue, because without it we cannot advance a step in the spiritual life. But our Father is well aware of our weakness. He knows that we are all proud, full of self-conceit . . . . "

Dom Helder is silent for a while. Then, with a rising inflexion, he continues:

"Someone who influenced me greatly in my Seminary days was Jackson de Figueiredo. I considered myself a Jacksonist. I absorbed his books and articles. Every issue of *A Ordem* I read avidly . . . .

"When Jackson died in a boating accident in 1928 Cardinal Leme chose Alceu Amoroso Lima, a young journalist, to succeed him. I wrote Alceu, sad about the loss of Jackson, but enthusiastic about his own appointment. He replied in his own handwriting and asked me to get in touch with a young army officer, Severino Sombra, who had been a friend of Jackson and was soon to take up a commission in Fortaleza. He asked me to work with him . . . . When Severino came to Fortaleza he put into practice the right-wing doctrine of his military college. To counteract the influence of communism he founded a league of rural and urban workers—Liga Cearense de Opararios, its members to be indoctrinated in Christian principles and organized to demand better working and living conditions. Similar organizations were set up in other cities in the Northeast . . . .

"As a Seminarian I enrolled as a volunteer 'Missionary of Work' and helped him to propagate the spiritual and social doctrine of the League. I even sewed the badge of a 'Missionary of Work', a worker's arm holding up a scales, on the sleeves of my cassock! When another young lieutenant, a friend of Severinos—Jeova Mota—came to Fortaleza he asked me to instruct him in the faith. He was received into the Church and in January 1930 Severino, Jeova and I set up the Centro Jackson de Figueiredo in Fortaleza, a counterpart, we hoped, of the Centro Dom Vital in Rio . . . .

"The weak point in my Seminary formation was the social part. During my time there, not a single professor was moved by the great human problems . . . .

"I don't believe that the Military School of Realengo could have given Severino Sombra any better social formation than the Seminary of Fortaleza gave to me . . . . In fact, the Seminary was unable to give me any wide or firmly based social vision. On the contrary, I left there seeing Communism as the evil of the century, the evil of evils, evil itself. To accept and defend the established 'order' and authority seemed to be my duty as a man and a Christian".

On May 24, 1932 Plinio Salgado founded the Brazilian Integralist Party. Brazil's Integralists openly imitated the European fascist parties. There was a symbol (the Sigma), a flag, members wore green shirts with black or white pants, they raised their right arm in the fascist salute. Their motto was "God, Country, Family". They preached a highly mystic form of nationalism, striving for a state that would honour both divine teaching, as expressed by the Catholic Church, and Brazilian inspirations. Plinio recognized a similarity in ideology and aims between his movement and the 'Liga Cearense de Operários'. As self-proclaimed National Chief he wrote to Severino, asking him to become Provincial Chief of the Northeast, with Padre Helder as educational secretary of the Province.[4]

6

The caring pastor

After breakfast this morning we leave for the diocesan offices. Dom Helder as a 'bishop of the poor' has no car, but we hardly walk a few yards when a car pulls up beside us, a long black American limousine, and the owner pulls down the window.

"A lift, Dom Helder?"

Dom Helder gestures me into the car. Dom Helder and his escort, a business man, talk animatedly all the way to the city centre. I can't follow the conversation which is in Portuguese, but the rapport between them is evident. No barriers separate the tones of voice, the gestures, the glances, the genuine interest. I follow an exchange that needs no words. We negotiate crowded city streets and turn into a narrow crowded road and pull up on the left hand side outside steps leading into the diocesan offices.

"Good-bye, Dom Helder".

"Good-bye, my friend, and thank you".

The business man waves and pulls away. No-one calls Dom Helder Archbishop or Monseignor. As we enter the building Dom Helder is stopped by a young man and almost immediately engulfed by a waiting group of people. The hall is wide and spacious, knots of people sitting or standing talking in groups. There is a constant passage of persons in and out of doors leading off the hall. Dom Helder disappears into a room on the right. A tall figure emerges from the room and approaches me. A serene face, a quiet spoken man, he introduces himself as Dom José Lamartine Soares, Dom Helder's auxiliary bishop. I know that in this large problematical archdiocese he is Dom Helder's right-hand man and support. We go into another room and he explains, in answer to my questions, how the diocese is administered. Dom Helder's organizational skill is in evidence:

"The work is organized between Dom Helder, myself, the

vicar-general and the elected episcopal vicars. There is also a council of priests . . . . "

Later in the morning as we re-enter the entrance hall I see Dom Helder in conversation with a tall priest. His progress across the room is slowed by the few words and gestures he bestows on each one he passes. He seems to know each one by name and circumstance; an encouraging word for the mother, an abraço for the delicate-looking baby in her arms, and a smile and pat on the head for the boy at her skirt. I notice the unobstrusive gesture with which he presses something into her hand and the gratitude in her eyes. He seems fatigued as he joins me but his eyes brighten, as if to order.

"Come, let us have some lunch and then we can talk".

Lunch, always a brief affair, is soon over and we settle down to another session.

"I was ordained a priest in the Cathedral of Fortaleza on August 15, 1931. The next morning I celebrated my first Mass. My servers at the altar were two young lieutenants in uniform—Severino Sombra and Jeova Mota. After the Mass they held my hands up to be kissed by the members of my family and the congregation. Since that day I have never separated God from my neighbour. I lived my priesthood with very deep emotion. It has fulfilled all my dreams of belonging to God and to others . . . . Monseignor Braga, the Vicar General, asked me to stay in the city to organize associations of workers, teachers and young people. The Archbishop also asked me to look after the chapel of a poor neighbourhood called Piedade, so that someday it might become a parish. All my work was done with the blessing of the Bishop, whom I obeyed blindly . . . . "

Dom Helder's face is serious.

"I continued to work with Severino and Jeova and their friends in their political organizations, and they helped me with my associations. We set up a youth group called Young Catholic Workers, after the European organization founded by Pere Cardijn. We gave the name to a huge band of poor children to whom we offered religious instruction, night school and games. Cardijn, who later became my close friend, laughed heartily at the idea. We also founded 'unions'. Having heard of trade unions, we organized Catholic trade unions of washer-women and domestics, which were no more than associations providing Christian education and self-help . . . .

"I worked with the teachers and established a Catholic Teachers' League. I became its first president, and Severino

Sombra became vice-president. We organized lectures, a series of conferences and discussions for the teachers and the students from the Teacher Training College . . . .

"We went to Rio with a group of teachers to attend the First National Congress of the Catholic Conference of Brazilian Educators (CCBE). Next I organized a Regional Congress of Catholic Educators at Baturiti in the Northeast. I became its chairman and also president of the Regional CCBE . . . ."

A long pause as Dom Helder reflects.

"When I was ordained a priest in 1931 I was under the impression that the world was going to divide itself in two—communism and anti-communism. I did not hesitate. I took my side: anti-communism. At that time I had an integralist soul. When Plinio Salgado, the founder of the Integralists, asked me to become Provincial Educational Secretary for the movement I took the invitation and the Integralist Manifesto and some articles by Plinio to my Bishop, Dom Manuel da Silva Gomes. I expressed my uneasiness about some aspects of the movement and the oath of allegiance to the National Chief. Dom Manuel decided that I should accept Plinio's offer. I made speeches and encouraged the movement in the diocese and I also wrote articles in the local newspaper *O Nordeste* in praise of the Integralists, and the role of the Church in upholding the values of the movement . . . .

"Dom Manuel also asked me to conduct the Catholic Electoral League campaign in the diocese, so I went to the towns and the villages holding meetings and making speeches to explain LEC's programme for prohibition of divorce, religious instruction in the public schools, chaplains in the armed forces and other points. Twenty-four deputies were elected in the Ceara area and nationwide Cardinal Leme's plan was very successful. The new assembly was sympathetic to LEC's programme . . . .

"The new Governor persuaded the Bishop that I should become State Director of the Department of Education. I refused because I had no official credentials in education, and I didn't wish to hold a government post. But Dom Manuel insisted I accept and out of obedience I agreed, on condition that party politics did not interfere with my work. In turn, I promised not to allow Integralist party policies to influence my decisions . . . .

"At 26 I became State Director of Education. A year later I had to resign because political pressures became too great. The very day I resigned an invitation arrived from a friend in Rio,

Lourenco Filho—who knew the pressures from experience—to join the Secretariate of Education of the Federal District in Rio de Janeiro as Technical Assistant. To avoid friction with the Governor, my bishop allowed me to leave. I left my beloved Ceara and the Northeast with his blessing. Ceara is not exchanged for anything except Heaven. I am, and always will be, a Nordestino''.

The term Catholic Action made popular by Pope Pius X (1903-1914) refers to the organized involvement of lay Catholics in the apostolic and pastoral life of the Church. For many centuries lay membership of the Church demanded little more than a passive assent to Catholic dogma, attendance at some church services and the occasional reception of the sacraments of penance and eucharist.

The lay apostolate movement which developed in the Church during the early 20th century stressed the importance of a deeper, more internalized religious commitment for all Catholics. It also promoted an extension of the influence of religion into areas of life and of society previously regarded as "profane" or "worldly", e.g. business, recreation, politics, social change.[5]

7

A new vision

"To-day we go to a celebration. My friend and co-worker Antonio has had a son after many years. The whole family rejoices to-day after the baptism and we will join them . . . . "

Antonio's friend calls for us and we drive to an area on the outskirts of the city where we turn off the main road into a rough track. Progress becomes slow and bumpy, gears are shifted and the car is enveloped in swirls of dust. As we approach groups of unostentatious new houses, children begin to run towards the car, and by the time we halt on an open space, as if by a secret signal a welcoming committee is there to greet Dom Helder. Men, women and children all gather round him smiling and happy, and the procession moves towards some houses further on from which sounds of samba music can be heard. The children run and skip around Dom Helder, dart back to look at the stranger, then off again in spurts of dust. Each house we pass has a minuscule front garden, and as we approach two adjoining houses at the end of the track, I see that their gardens are filled with young men and women dancing to the music in concentric circles in the congested space. Antonio and a group of men come forward to welcome Dom Helder, and I am introduced as a friend from Ireland.

Above the noise of the dancing:
"Holland?"
"No! Ireland".
"Ah! England".
"No! Ireland".
And Dom Helder launches into an explanation in Portuguese.

Antonio propels Dom Helder through the garden gate, and we file into the tiny house along a passage into a room with a laden table. Then into the room where the mother and child are enthroned surrounded by a group of women. Dom Helder embraces them all, takes the child in his arms and kisses it and his running commentary, while rocking the baby, evokes an instant response and much laughter from the group. He passes him to me, a tiny scrap of humanity with solemn beautiful brown eyes oblivious to the arms of a stranger and the noisy chatter, the music and laughter around him. I go to sit beside his mother and continue to hold and admire this much longed for son of Antonio. I have no language problems here as the baby responds to my tone of voice seeming content, and I am spared any faltering attempts at Portuguese with the adults. The room becomes more crowded as guests continue to arrive. I am persuaded to join the dancing outside, so relinquishing the child to its mother. I go out into the cooler evening air and find Dom Helder already part of the group of dancers. I join in readily, encouraged by the spectators outside the garden, whose numbers are also swelling. The rest of the visit alternates between dancing periods outdoors and incursions to rest indoors where I dodge pressing invitations to have more. I notice Dom Helder at times in serious conversation with Antonio and his friends, and again laughing and joking with others. He comes towards me.

"We go now to inspect the new centre".

We say farewell to the family with many abraços. The sound of dancing and festivity follows us over the uneven ground as, led by Antonio and some of his friends, we approach a low cemented building. Our arrival at the door is heralded by a group of children and their two teachers. They have interrupted their lessons to welcome Dom Helder. He asks many questions and listens attentively. The volunteer teachers are the first group to function in the multi-purpose building erected by the children's fathers as part of a self-help scheme. The teachers and children join us as we visit the other rooms, mostly unfurnished except for the dentist's surgery where expensive dental equipment—a donation to Dom Helder from overseas—is partly unpacked. Dom Helder sits in the dentist's chair and laughingly tilts his head back and opens his mouth much to the delight of the surrounding urchins. We complete our tour and it is time to leave. More abraços, much waving of hands and exhortations as we drive away in a cloud of dust.

At home once more, he continues his narration:

"On January 16, 1936 I arrived in Rio. I stayed in a boarding house run by a lady from Ceara and later when my father and my unmarried sister, Nair, moved to Rio I lived with them . . . .

"I became a student once again and sat for the Ministry of Education examination to become an 'Expert in Education'. I passed the examination and took up my post at the Federal Ministry as technical assistant to Lourenco Filho . . . .

"Cardinal Leme asked me to help in the revision of the teaching of religion and to lecture on psychology at the new Catholic Faculty of Philosophy. I pleaded my lack of experience but to no avail. I often say the only University degrees I have, I got through the window, not the door . . . .

"I was Chaplain to a community of Sisters and gave retreats, heard confessions, and preached in the city churches. I spent 7 years at the Federal Ministry of Education, first as technical assistant and then as head of the Programs and Examinations of the Institute for Educational Research, looking after public elementary day schools. I found the work boring, dealing with bureaucrats and bureaucracy. I wanted so much to be more involved in the priestly ministry. I begged for permission to go to the rural areas of Brazil, as a missionary, to set up catechetical programmes. But the Cardinal thought it more important to have a priest in the Education Ministry. He felt that I could do a lot of good and have an influence, just by being there . . . .

"When I first came to the Archdiocese of Rio I had to ask the Cardinal for permission to exercise my priestly faculties. He was very happy to have me in the Archdiocese, but on one condition —I must give up integralism and all my political activities. Dom Manuel had been instrumental in my involvement in the movement and I obeyed. Dom Leme asked me to leave it and I obeyed . . . .

When Dom Leme wanted me out of integralism, obedience and my serious doubts about totalitarianism made me accept . . .

"Away from politics during my years at the Federal Ministry, I had time to reflect on the political involvement into which my anti-communism had drawn me. I read avidly and discussed with friends the ideas and thoughts of theologians of the day. I came especially under the influence of that great Catholic philosopher and writer, Jacques Maritain, who had visited the Centro Dom Vital . . . .

"With my friend and mentor Alceu Amoroso Lima of the Centro, I began to see and understand Maritain's liberating political and social philosophy, and that to believe all anti-communist forces were allies of the Church was wrong. Fascism could be just as dangerous as communism. I began to realize the fallacy of my capitalism-communism dichotomy. The greatest enemy of the Church was not communism but the factors that led the masses to embrace communism—religious ignorance, economic deprivation and political powerlessness''.

All observers of Dom Helder have noted his charismatic capacity to stimulate, innovate and inspire. He could exercise these gifts to the full in Rio, for he was auxiliary bishop and thus without the fixed pastoral duties of an ordinary. After founding the National Conference of Bishops of Brazil (CNBB) in 1952, he was able to devote much of his time to its growth and development . . . . the Church was confronted by threats of various kinds and the Cardinal and other bishops allowed Dom Helder considerable leeway in forming a response. He directed this response through the CNBB, thereby institutionalizing what could have remained a very personal programme or movement.[6]

8.

The Reformer begins

"When Cardinal Leme died in 1942 he was succeeded by Dom Jaime de Barros Camara. He freed me from my desk work at the Federal Bureau and appointed me Vice-director of Catechetics in the Archdiocese. My archbishop was a traditionalist and very anti-communist. I had to carry out my new assignment on traditional lines, catechesis meaning rote learning. We held 'catechetical marathons' with every diocese sending two candidates in four age groups to Rio for written or oral tests. The winners went to Rome for the Holy Year. Only gradually was I able to move away from such methods to a more christo-centric approach . . . .

"I was also the Diocesan Chaplain to Catholic Action (AC) in Rio, and later I became National Vice-Chaplain to the movement. I had to organize meetings at local and provincial level, prepare papers, plans, and reports for the AC week-long National Congress which was held every year.

"My work with AC took me across the whole country and I met bishops and priests, people of all ages and walks of life and learnt about the Church and its place or non-place in Brazilian life. During those years, the '50s, two efforts were made to reform the AC movement to gain some measure of autonomy for the diocesan chaplains and branches. But the more the laity became organized and involved in the apostolate the more AC seemed to pose a threat to clerical dominance. Many of the bishops were unhappy about the new shape of AC in their diocese, where each bishop functioned like a feudal lord . . . . You know Brazil is a very big country, as big as the whole of America minus Alaska. At that time the bishops in the South below Rio de Janeiro knew very little of the problems of the people or the Church in the Northeast. In the South were the rich farmlands and ranches and great wealth, in the North terrible poverty. I thought, Ah! we must bring the bishops together to share the problems of our country . . . .

"When the Nuncio, Archbishop Carlo Chiarlo, came to Rio in 1946 he asked me to come and see him each week and tell him about Brazil and the Church. Every Saturday I went to the Nunciature for a meeting with the Nuncio and then we would have lunch together. I told him of the need to set up a national organization for the Bishops, with a secretariate and experts to study the problems of the Church and the country . . . .

"In 1950 because of my work in Rio I made my first visit to Rome to attend the World Congress for the teaching of religion. The following year I went to attend the World Congress of the Lay Apostolate, and after consultation with the Nuncio, and with his blessing, I took along the proposals for a national conference of Bishops and a letter of introduction to Monseignor Montini, Secretary of State. I left the proposals with the Secretary, who said he would study them and send for me . . . .

"There is a great difference in climate between Rome in winter and Recife. I was staying in very cold lodgings and the day Monseignor Montini sent for me I had lost my hearing so I turned, as I often do, to my guardian angel. I call him Jose—my mother's pet name for me as a child—and I asked him to see to it that the Secretary would understand my French and that I would be able to hear on this important occasion . . . . "

A big grin appears on Dom Helder's face.

"I suppose I didn't look much like a Monseignor because the Vatican officials refused to accept my story of an appointment. Eventually all was solved and I got to the Secretary. He agreed with the proposals to set up the Bishops Conference, but he had one question, 'How will the Bishops of Brazil accept the fact that you have worked out this scheme and should set it up, but you are not a bishop?'

Did the Secretary of State think I wanted to be a bishop? 'Monseignor, I am a simple priest and I only wish to serve God and the Church in Brazil. You too serve the Church in the important post of Secretary and you are not a bishop'.

"A year later the Nuncio sent me back to Rome, and when I met the Secretary of State once again he promised the Conference would be born in a few months. The National Conference of the Bishops of Brazil was created in Rio in October 1952 and I was named Secretary General, and remained so until 1964.

"Six sub-secretariates were set up: Education, Social Action, Doctrine, Seminaries and Vocations, Catholic Action and the Catholic Electoral League.

"A monthly bulletin was produced and circulated to the Bishops, and we held the first meeting of CNBB at Belem in 1953. At first only the Cardinals and Archbishops could take part in the discussions and vote, but at the second meeting it was decided that all the bishops could do so".

Here Dom Helder smiles.

"Even bishops can grow in democracy!"

"The Church found it imperative to launch in Rio an urbanization campaign for the favelas of the Capital . . . for two main reasons: the subhuman situation of the favela dwellers, living as they do in shacks without water, without light, without sanitation, in a state of misery even more shocking because of the beauty of the city and its material progress; and because for those very reasons the Rio favelas have become centres of dangerous social agitation, especially as a result of Communist exploitation . . . . [7]

9

Help for the helpless

After supper as the sky darkens we set off for one of the favelas. Dom Helder locks the little wooden door and as we walk past the church a VW taxi draws up beside us. VW taxis are a species of their own in Brazil. This one is yellow, left hand drive and, as is usual, the seat beside the driver removed for easier passenger access. Dom Helder enters first and sits behind the driver. They converse through the mirror for a while, and then I notice Dom Helder's head nodding and soon he is asleep. I brace myself each time the taxi screeches to a halt to prevent shooting towards the window across the empty space in front. Dom Helder sleeps on placidly.

I notice we travel from the city centre out towards its fringes, the journey here a reverse of the usual transition from crowded city centre to suburbs. We pass from the most expensive hotels in the world on the magnificent sea front inwards past select condominiums and residential areas, banks, shopping centres, less spectacular housing and now we are on a wide road lined with palm trees and scattered houses. The taxi begins to hump and jolt and finally comes to a halt. Dom Helder awakes and as he steps out of the taxi seems to take for granted that the road has petered out at the edge of a slope.

Down below clinging to the slopes I see a collection of huts and shacks lit by looped naked electric light bulbs. As I look, Dom Helder who has already begun to descend the slope signals to me to follow, and as I do, out of the shadows come figures in twos and threes and converge on Dom Helder. Mothers clutching children, fathers, boys and girls follow the tiny figure. I am reminded of the Pied Piper of Hamelin as I negotiate planks placed over open drains between narrow lines of shacks leaning against each other. My foot slips off the plank into the drain. I withdraw a shoeless foot. There is nothing to do but fumble for it, empty it and put it on. It is no longer white! I hurry to rejoin the train of people which is squeezing its way into a low cemented building with small windows. Every seat is filled by women and children, most of the men standing around the walls. In front of the group Dom Helder sits at a table set with papers, flanked by two men. A young man, obviously an American, comes forward, introduces himself as a Peace Corps worker and leads me to a chair near the table. The young American sits beside me and explains.

"The man on Dom Helder's right is Chairman of the Committee. They have asked Dom Helder to come and speak to them. There is a division among the favelados about a well for the favela". The Chairman, after a few words with Dom Helder, stands up and speaks to the group. Then it is Dom Helder's turn. He stands up and walks around to the front of the table. His face comes alive and he begins to speak. He gestures to the wall on his left and, still talking, walks over to it and bends his head and appears to be pulling something from the wall and eating it, with one arm sticking out behind him. As I watch him fascinated the Peace Corps worker whispers in my ear, "He's dramatizing the fable of the two donkeys tied together who want to satisfy their hunger at opposite sides of the field".

Dom Helder rushes to the other wall, his long black cassock trailing on the floor. I think to myself he must be losing weight. He repeats the performance on the other side and then slowly returns to the centre of the room and sits on the floor and chews contentedly. He rises and addresses the favelados once again. My interpreter:

"He's urging them to join together and ask for a well; he's asking them to sign the sheet of paper on the table".

A woman raises her hand. My interpreter continues:

"She's asking what will happen to the men who sign. In another favela the police came with the list and took the men away from their families. Dom Helder is telling them they must have hope. They must ask for themselves because they need running water for themselves and their children for reasons of health. In another favela they did get their well, in another a road was built. Dom Helder is asking who will sign the petition".

Slowly a few hands are raised, the women urge the men and a few more come forward. By now the air is stifling and the children increasingly restless. The signing over, the crowd spills out into the night with Dom Helder at its centre, and we are escorted to the road. A friend of Dom Helder's is waiting to drive us home. Dom Helder falls silent after a while, then he turns to me.

"My people! Some of them don't even have hope. It is hard to make them understand but I must keep on trying".

He looks sad and tired as we embrace and say 'Good-night'.

His friend drives me home to Madalena.

A welcome surprise in my room—and I run to clasp the lost suitcase, search for the keys and open it. Five, six, seven—all the tapes are safe. Deo gratias!

We thank Cardinal Jaime Camara for the zeal of the Cruzada Sao Sebastiao which is doing so much to save from material and moral misery hundreds of thousands of Brazilians, among whom are numerous Nordestinos; but we denounce the actual exodus of Nordestinos as less a migration than a rout for they go, exploited by middlemen, with the minimum of material resources; without documents, without special preparation, without equipment, without a destination; without any form of special assistance; to end up in the favelas of Rio or, at best, as a sub-proletariat of the South.[8]

10

A growing ministry

Early next morning we wait for a friend of Dom Helder's to take us to Manguinhos, the ex-Episcopal palace. Dom Helder continues to use a few rooms in Manguinhos, where crowds constantly come for a few words with him. While we wait I ask him about the Congress.

"In 1952 Dom Jaime asked me to organize the 36th International Eucharistic Congress to be held in Rio in three years time. We had to prepare the design and security of the site; calculate the number of visitors; the accommodation needed; the food and water supplies; traffic control; publicity and press facilities. I had many helpers from Catholic Action, even in the Government, and we had eleven commissions looking after the various sectors . . . .

"In the huge Maracana football stadium there were 200,000 people assembled for the beginning of the Eucharistic Year, and everything was a success. We had few problems despite the fears. God was with us because we did it all to honour Christ . . . .

"I think my Cardinal was worried about all the attention given to me at that time. He cared for me like a father and was afraid all the notice and fuss I got would go to my head. One day I brought him a book I had written on prayer and the presence of God. It reassured him. He wanted me to remain humble and simple . . . .

"In 1955 I was named Auxiliary Archbishop of Rio. I had been involved with the press and radio during the preparations for the Congress, and I continued to use the media as a means of reaching the people with a radio programme each evening at eight . . . .

"After the Congress 100 bishops from Latin America remained in Rio for a 10-day Conference. As Secretary General of CNBB I had made all the arrangements in advance, and I put these bishops including the dignitaries from Rome all in the same building on their arrival in Rio, so they knew each other before the Conference started. We discussed the major problems of the Church in Latin America, spiritual and social, and at the end of two weeks the bishops voted unanimously to create a permanent Conference for Latin American bishops. Rome approved the idea and Bogota, Colombia, was decided as the venue. And so CELAM was born, Dom Jaime became its first President and I served three terms as Vice-President . . . .

"After the Congress Cardinal Gerlier of Lyons came to see me. He congratulated me on the success of the Congress and praised my organizational ability, but then he said, 'Why don't you use this ability to find a solution for the favelas, the scandal of this beautiful city . . . . '

"The word favela means flower and these slums are like an obscene growth on the fringes of steep hills. Sometimes the policy is to raze them to the ground by fire or bulldozer so that the people are forced to leave. Favelas are growing around many of the big cities due to the misery of the peasants migrating from the rural areas. The people live in shacks made of cardboard or crates, with roofs made of Coca-Cola tins or corrugated iron— no running water, no light. As President of the Catholic Migration Commission I had been well aware of the problem but I hadn't been involved in the battle. During the Congress Christ had been honoured in the Eucharist, now I was determined to honour him in the poor . . . .

"My traditional Cardinal was fearful of my getting involved in the struggle. He was uncertain about the new social trend in AC and in the Church, but he reluctantly agreed. We had over a hundred favelas in Rio with some 400,000 people. I had the plan to build apartment blocks with a church, a school, parent-teacher association, social workers and a residents' council, and gradually re-house the favelados. Members of AC and CNBB, radio and T.V. and contacts who had helped with the Congress collaborated in the scheme. The Government provided a plot of land for an industrial zone. The idea was that factories built on the plot would provide rent for the project. I called the scheme Cruzada Sao Sebastiao. In three years the completed buildings housed almost a thousand families, the school had 600 pupils, very good teachers, the adults had classes in hygiene, child care and professional training . . . . In addition, the Rio city merchants and co-operatives financed a perishable goods depot and market".

Dom Helder smiles in remembrance.

"When I told Pope John XXIII about the Cruzada he thought the name was an unhappy one. It was a foolish choice of mine, with its memories of Crusade times . . . .

"Ah! yes, and the Banco da Providencia. It was St. Vincent de Paul who said, 'We must conquer by love the right to give'. We must get rid of every idea of alms. He who is helped today, is helped with the conviction that tomorrow he will be able to help. And so we organized a Feira da Providencia and asked everyone to send things for sale at the fair. All the states sent produce, even countries outside Brazil. Every year we have a fair, and this year it made a profit of one million dollars. You have met Cecelia, my devoted secretary of 26 years. She is President of the Banco. It funds hundreds of projects, children's homes, health clinics, even a rehabilitation service for prostitutes. It goes collateral for low interest loans from commercial banks for poor people . . . .

"We ran into many problems because we were dealing with human beings. The true cause of the favelas is in the countryside, the need for land reform. The Cruzada was only an emergency service. It didn't go to the root. It called attention to the problem".

Make Me a Rainbow

which brings together all the colours
into which your light
is fragmented!
Make me, even more
a rainbow
which announces the calm
after the storm.[9]

11

The man of prayer

"Dom Helder, how can I get closest to understanding the spirit that inspires you?"

It is now 6 p.m. and we have just returned from one of our visits to the favelas. I look at this little man from whom life seems to have ebbed. His face is pale and drawn, his clerical collar loosened, his hands resting on the table as if for support. Visiting the people of the favela his whole person had displayed the urgency of his message of hope: flashing eyes, dramatic gestures, a constant flow of words of encouragement. When we returned home I had suggested we skip our session for the evening, but Dom Helder refused. Now as he gathers his thoughts together he suddenly comes alive again, straightens his shoulders and answers.

"The essence of Dom Helder is in his meditations, they are the most intimate and profound records of my heart. I write them during the early morning hours".

He reiterates with typical Dom Helder repetitiveness and rising inflexions:

"It is there that you will discover truly, truly, truly—Dom Helder. As a young priest—ordained at 22½ years by special permission from Rome—my aim was to be devoured by my people. I understood from the beginning that I would need a close relationship with God in order to have something of value to share with others . . . .

"From my youth I have had the ability to rise early from sleep, and as a priest, I make a practice of rising each morning at 2 a.m. and spending some hours in prayer. At present my routine as you know is to retire at 10.30 p.m., rise at 2 a.m., spend from 2 till 4 a.m. in prayer and preparation of work, sleep again from 4 a.m. to 5 a.m., rise, shower and celebrate Mass at 6 a.m. . . . .

"I begin by saying my breviary in a very simple way. I open the window, look at the sky, read the psalms, and review the day that has passed. I recall all those I met, the people I have seen; the news I have heard of the city, the nation, the world, interests me enormously. When I meet a person the meeting is on a very personal level. If that person is Irish like yourself I think of Ireland and its problems, and I think of all the people of all religions who are doing so much good for the world. During the day, perhaps, I meet a worker, Antonio . . . . I think of all the workers everywhere in the world . . . . His wife is pregnant: . . . . I think of all the women in the world who are expecting a son.

"When I meet a person bent under suffering I have the liberty and freedom to think: 'Lord, I know you have no need of Pere Jose. I know, I know it very well. But you have a daughter, Marguerite, who is broken and burdened . . . . It is necessary to hear her because her state is unbelievable'. I think the good Lord likes this counsel, this liberty, and confidence.

"I consider there is no need of words to talk with God so I think to myself, 'Lord, I would like to lend you my eyes, ears, mouth and hands. Look through my eyes, listen through my ears, and speak through my mouth'. It is so good, so good to look at the world, at mankind, when one lends one's ears to Christ. There is never a possibility for hatred, never a possibility but to love, to love largely, grandly, fully. Even when applause attends my efforts it is easy to defend myself. I think—very soft and low—'Lord, I know the little donkey which brought you on your triumphant journey to Jerusalem. It makes me happy that I can carry Christ to the world' . . . .

"My night vigil is also a time for work, and sometimes a longer vigil is necessary. Tonight I must work from midnight to 5 a.m. because I have among other things an important letter to prepare. I must write to Dominique de Menuil, widow of John de Menuil from Houston, Texas . . . . Mr. and Mrs. Menuil built an ecumenical chapel at Houston and they wished to hold a special ceremony there on 6 December to celebrate the 25th anniversary of the universal declaration of Human Rights. I suggested a presentation in music and dance illustrating the 'Suffering World': the suffering that exists in the world to be enacted in such a way as to pinpoint for people of goodwill the grave problems of life not only in Asia, Africa and South America, but also the inhuman state of the poor and under-privileged in rich industrialized nations. About three weeks before he died, John asked me to comfort and help his wife, and his secretary of many years. Dominique has now written to me to say that there would be grave technical difficulties about such a presentation, suggesting instead that three or four speakers, including myself, assemble there to speak together and later declare publicly how we see the world and the task of helping the world . . . .

"Tonight I must write my reply to her letter . . . . After that I must prepare a conference for the young Cardinal of Sao Paulo—Paulo Evaristo Arns . . . . One of my greatest joys is counting such a first-class member of the Brazilian episcopacy among my friends. He has asked me to speak during a week of conferences on human rights, at the Pontifical Catholic University of Sao Paulo . . . . Such is my life . . . . prayer and work".

Do the shacks in which they live deserve the name of house? Is what they eat nourishment? Are the rags they wear clothes? Can the situation in which they vegetate, without health, without expectations, without vision, without ideals be called life? . . . . Christianity is not content with your alms—it demands from you justice for your workers . . . .

Why is the Church getting involved in these questions which are economic rather than spiritual? . . . . These are human problems and the human person is one and indivisible; it is the moral law which is violated when the fundamental rights of the person are threatened or ignored . . . . [10]

"I have been devoting my time to the problems of the Northeast, already at 8.00 a.m. requesting Dom Helder to supply me with the documentation of the proposals approved at the Meeting . . . . conferring with my ministers and experts . . . . Dom Helder, although not a part of the administration nor of office, did not spare his collaboration and help. His voice is always listened to in government counsels on account of his generous public spirit and his role as representative of the bishops of the Northeast". [11]

12

A bishop's plight

This afternoon I choose the chair on Dom Helder's left. These tropical days in Recife I am wearing sleeveless dresses and I find that Dom Helder's enthusiastic emphasis on my sunburnt upper arm leaving its mark. Yesterday the left arm had its share!

"In 1956 as Secretary of CNBB and with the support of the Nuncio we called the first Meeting of Bishops of the Northeast to discuss the problems of the area. It was also a problem area for the government so I asked the new President Juscelino Kubitschek to attend, and he agreed. We had two meetings with government administrators and ministers at the Presidential Palace before the meeting, and we prepared a dossier for the bishops' assembly to which representatives from the ministries and agencies also came. At its conclusion a 'Declaration' was issued, in which the bishops placed themselves very firmly on the side of the poor and exploited, and asked the President for a national programme to help the Northeast . . . .

"Later that year he called the bishops to a press conference at the Presidential Palace and threatened to fire members of the federal agencies who couldn't produce concrete action in the Northeast. A very severe drought in 1958 finally generated the national programme . . . .

"Kubitschek sent to Congress a law creating a Superintendency for the Development of the Northeast. It met with opposition because of vested interests. CNBB met on May 24-26, '59 in Natal and the President, opening the session which was also attended by the Nuncio, spoke of the bill and of the initiative of the bishops in the problems of the Northeast. The bishops acclaimed the President's new bill. Next day it was passed and became law by the end of the year.

"When CNBB was founded in 1952, ACB (Catholic Action

Brazil) became one of its departments.

"My work as ACB National Chaplain made me aware of the grave social problems of Brazil, particularly in the rural areas. AC organized courses for rural priests in co-operation with the Agriculture and Education Ministries. Teams were set up (a priest, doctor, agronomist, veterinarian, teacher and a social worker) to train local people to tackle local problems. Gradually the bishops in many dioceses became involved in the work, and also the Nuncio. The biggest problem was that millions of rural workers had no land at all . . . .

"As Secretary of CNBB Msgr. Montini, Papal Secretary of State, had sent me a letter concerning land reform in Brazil and requesting a statement from the bishops. Land reform was put on the agenda for our meetings. Many of the bishops themselves owned huge land properties, and most members of Congress were landowners, so land reform of any kind was very difficult . . . .

"AC members, especially the University students, wanted to be part of the action for social change. They saw radical agrarian reform as one of the main solutions for the underdevelopment of Brazil, but many prominent laymen and some of the bishops reacted to these radical and 'Communist' trends. I myself was labelled 'Red' and 'Communist' . . . .

"I had to present the viewpoints of the Episcopal Commission of ACB to the members, and at the same time try to explain the ideals and frustrations of the militants to the Commission. When my second six-year term as National Chaplain came to an end I was not re-appointed, but as Secretary General of CNBB I continued to try and keep the dialogue going between the two sides. Many AC members dropped out, but many continued to be involved in two of CNBB's movements—the Rural Unions and the basic education movement (MEB) . . . .

"I know Marina Bandeira has told you MEB's lifestory. She had been my director of publicity for the Eucharistic Congress and later became executive secretary of the National Association of Catholic Radio Stations (RENEC). Its aim was the establishment of radio schools in the North and Northeast. Training schemes and programmes were so successful that soon the schools were attracting the attention of the Government. After consultation with the bishops, the new president Janio Quadros signed a decree inaugurating Movimento Educacao de Base (MEB) in 1961.

"CNBB was to set up at least 1500 radio schools each year

and train personnel nationwide, and the government was to fund the movement for 5 years. Marina became General Secretary of MEB. In its initial stages the movement aimed at wiping out illiteracy as more than 60% of the adult population in the North, Northeast and Centrewest couldn't read or write. But gradually, with the new social thinking prevailing among many of the leaders, especially those of AC, the movement began to incorporate local community meetings into the programme. The radio classes developed into group discussions of the programmes, and the actual life of the participants was examined as a method of conscientization. Ideas such as those of my good friend, Recife's educator Paulo Freire, were explored and the peasants helped to discover the reality of their position. People in a situation of dependence—but also people with the freedom, the hope to change that situation. MEB's new text-books explained these ideas as did the broadcast programmes . . . .

"Some of the bishops were uneasy about MEB's new orientation, but in 1963 during the second session of Vatican Council II with all the emphasis on the place of the people in the Church, especially the Decree on the Apostolate of the Laity, they voted to make RENEC an autonomous body and no longer under the wing of CNBB. Marina Bandeira became its first lay President . . . .

"The following year a military coup brought down the Government. Conservative forces in State and Church united in reaction for the 'good of the country'. Many of the leaders of AC, MEB and the Rural Unions were jailed. MEB's new primer, *Viver é Lutar* (To Live is to Fight) was seized and confiscated".

DIDST THINK I WAS UNAWARE?

When everything and everybody seemed remote,
When my fatigue was overwhelming,
When difficulties loomed up everywhere,
A puff of air came through the open window,
Sent by thee, and gently stroked my face.[12]

13

A rose by any name

We are standing in Dom Helder's 10' x 12' garden and I am about to leave for Madalena. We have been speaking about creation and nature. Dom Helder now points to the solitary rambling rose that has struggled to look over one of the high white walls enclosing his garden between the church, the street and the neighbouring house.

"You know imagination is very important in understanding creation, it helps us to understand God. Once when the ants had eaten the leaves of my rose-bush I picked up an ant and scolded it for doing so. But the ant in my palm taught me a lesson. As it squirmed in my hand it replied: 'Why should you be the only one to enjoy the rose-bush?' "

I am reminded of a story told to me by a Catholic sister working in Recife who had called to see Dom Helder about two urgent questions. One matter was discussed and settled, and then Dom Helder interjected:

"Do you know what happened last night? I came home and found my rose—my little Prince—stripped of leaves. I knew quite well who did it, so I picked up my little ant and talked to it. For a few minutes it wasn't listening and then I realized it was looking at the sky, which it was seeing for the first time. All her life that creature had never before seen the sky. When she had got over her wonder and I knew she would listen to me, I said, 'Roses are beautiful and you shouldn't harm them. You love me and I love you, but I also love the rose, and to strip it of leaves is very violent of you. I'm going to show you how to do something' "

"In Brazil they have a saying, 'I'm going to give you a smell'. It is a sign of affection, as when people meet and greet each other they press their cheeks together and kiss the air. All the time one sees this, as when mothers hold up their babies to be caressed. I held up the ant to the rose to show its affection, because it had never smelt a rose before. Ever since then there has been no problem, and the rose and the ant have lived together peacefully . . . . ''

On my way home I remember other instances. A first glimpse of Dom Helder at the airport in Washington, surrounded by a welcoming group of important officials. Suddenly he stops, the cortege also stops as Dom Helder smiles and waves at a beautiful flock of birds passing overhead . . . .

Dom Helder in the garden of a house about to be vacated by its occupants, bending over a flowering shrub and whispering— "I would love to come and live here because you are so beautiful but I really can't. Do you understand? Ah, good! . . . . ''

I remember him speaking so convincingly to me one day about his Guardian Angel that I instinctively looked around to where he was pointing as if to an unseen presence.

"He is my good friend and he is there especially in moments of great joy as in moments of greater suffering. At present I do not know his name, but one day, when I arrive in the abode of the Father, I will know by name him whom I now call by the name I like most—José—the same name my mother called me in moments when she was most content with me. This is why I have chosen José as the nom-de-plume for my meditations, my poems, the essence of my soul''.

His ability to pass easily from the natural to the supernatural gives him great consolation and great courage. I asked him once about living alone. His reply:

"One day, the Pope asked me if I did not run the risk of my life being in danger. I replied: 'Holy Father, I am absolutely convinced that the offering of my life for the good of the human race does not depend on me, but on Almighty God' ''.

Then striking one of his many dramatic attitudes he spoke to me directly:

"I cannot say to you, 'Look at me! You are face to face with a future martyr'. Ah no! But no! It must be a personal choice of the Father and no one can merit this personal grace. But if the Lord makes the choice—and if I should merit it—I am convinced that He will help me at the given moment''.

He continued:

"Very often I am questioned about living here all alone, especially during the night, opening the door myself to all the callers. It would be so easy to be killed, they say. My reply is always the same. 'But I do not live by myself'. 'Ah! yes . . . . So there is someone else here?' But certainly. There are three persons—the Father, the Son and Holy Spirit'. I enjoy all the current discussions of theologians very much, but I must admit I hold on to my own conception of the Blessed Trinity".

And here Dom Helder broke into peals of surprisingly strong infectious laughter to issue from such a frail body. Then, with a shining countenance and a gesture as if to encompass the world, he confounds all those who fear for his life.

"See! How I am protected! The three persons of the Blessed Trinity and José, mon Ange gardien! How easy it is for me to move between the visible and invisible worlds! I also have the little rose-bush in the garden out there, and like the rose of the Little Prince it says to me: 'I have four thorns to protect you. I see all who come in and I will defend you' "

With another swift change of mood:

"Defend me? . . . . Protect me? . . . . I think that perhaps the most protected person in the world was J. F. Kennedy . . . . If the Father should accept my life, I am ready . . . . I think it very important that a pastor be always ready to offer his life for his people".

Msgr. Helder Camara . . . . is one of the most astonishing personalities of the Council. His modesty keeps him from intervening on the Council floor but his influence is immense. Everyone at Rome knows that he is the bishop of the poor 'par excellence' . . . . The Pope has a special love for him; even better, Paul VI has told him personally of all the influence he has on him. That is why his proposals should be listened to with the greatest attention. There was a packed house at the Dutch Information Centre . . . . to hear his latest conference when he tackled the subject—at times incorrectly considered taboo as the Pope's preserve— the reform of the Curia. He did it as always in his own direct and daring style.[13]

14

The struggle for justice

"My ideas on social justice have travelled a long way since I was a young priest in Fortaleza . . . .

"In the '50s I became aware of the vast problems facing my country and the Church, the 'realidade Brasileira'. I began to understand that partial or local solutions were not the answer but a world awareness of the basic reason for the world's problems . . . .

"In September 1960 my Archbishop Cardinal Jaime Camara celebrated a special solemn Mass in the Candelaria Church in Rio for the Tricentenary of St. Vincent de Paul. He asked me to preach the sermon and I used the opportunity to show that if St. Vincent de Paul, the founder of those great missionaries of charity, were alive to-day his charity would be to work for justice. I pointed out that there was more poverty in the world than in St. Vincent's time three hundred years previously. Human beings were being crushed by both capitalist and communist regimes, yet Christians preferred to denounce Communism rather than misery and injustice . . . .

"Dom Jaime was known publicly for his denunciations of Communism on television. After my sermon that day in the Candelaria the difference in our thinking was evident. As a result many of my friends who supported the work of the Cruzada and the Banco withdrew their help. Dom Jaime had long had reservations about my work with Catholic Action, the Rural Unions and the favelas but he had always supported the programmes. However when MEB's new primer *Viver e Lutar* (To Live is to Fight) was seized by the Governor, Dom Jaime disclaimed publicly all responsibility for it. The time had come for us to part. Dom Jaime, who had always treated me honourably, spoke to me like a father, honestly and explicitly.

'My son, we must part as Paul and Barnabas did and remain brothers'.

"I accepted that it would be difficult to continue as his assistant and told him I was ready to serve in any diocese . . . .

"I went to Rome in March 1964 to work on one of the commissions preparing for the Third Session of the Council in September. While I was there the news arrived of the death of the archbishop of Recife. The Holy Father sent for me to offer me the vacant diocese. He saw it as a sign of Providence . . . . "

A long pause.

"Dom Helder, tell me about the Council?" . . . .

Another pause as Dom Helder collects his thoughts.

"When I remember the Council I remember a great saint— Pope John, the Peasant Pope, the Pope of the people. He was so human, so trusting, full of love for all mankind, with the simplicity of a true Christian. He had always shown an interest in our continent. Even before the Council he wrote many appeals to the bishops of Europe and North America to send people and help to Latin America . . . .

"I had the privilege of meeting with him three times. The first time in 1959 he opened his arms and said: 'I expected a great archbishop, all I see is a very little one'. We spoke with great openness as brothers about so many concerns; about what was close to our hearts, God's people, the problems in the world. He understood so well. He was truly the servant of the servants of God, not only for Christians but for all men everywhere. That's why he called Vatican Council II for dialogue, dialogue with all men. He opened the Second Vatican Council with words of encouragement, whatever had to be condemned had been condemned in the past. He wrote *Pacem in Terris* for 'all men of good will' . . . .

"I have known Pope Paul since 1951 when I went to Rome to ask for a Conference of Bishops in Brazil. In 1960 he came as Cardinal Montini to Rio and we visited the favelas together and he saw the misery of the poor . . . .

"I have had many private audiences with him since then. He had the same love of humanity as Pope John. He too wanted dialogue and peace. He wasn't afraid to dialogue with the communists in Milan where he was called the 'Red Archbishop'. They called him the same name in Rio. Remember it is Pope Paul who set up the Vatican Secretariate for non-Christian religions and the Secretariate for non-believers . . . .

"My greatest unhappiness would be to ever lose the

confidence of the Holy Father. At the Council I never spoke in the plenary sessions of the Assembly, never once. I was very angry sometimes listening to the speeches, but I remained silent . . . .

"I preferred to speak out in informal meetings with bishops from all over the world. One little ecumene was a group of Cardinals and bishops who were concerned that the Church be the Church of the poor, a servant Church. We held meetings right through the four sessions of the Council. At the beginning the group was small, at the end of the Council there were several hundred bishops and, I think, twelve Cardinals. There was another group who used to meet at Domus Mariae where many of us were staying during the Council. Cardinal Suenens had another group at the Belgian College. We were all concerned with the place of the Church in the world. I went to all the groups. I had discussions with theologians, experts, observers. I spoke with anyone who would speak with me about under-development, about the need for a theology of development. I longed for dialogue. The Council gave me many opportunities, meeting bishops from all over the world we could discuss our common problems. I found they were everywhere the same, two-thirds of the children of God living in hunger . . . .

"We worked in committees and commissions making drafts and amendments that resulted in the Council accepting the Pastoral Constitution of the Church in the Modern World. Listening to and talking with my brother bishops taught me about the Third World and the widespread injustice of the social system. The biblical meaning of the word 'world' where man has the duty to complete and improve creation for himself and his fellowmen—I resolved to work to make the whole world understand this . . . .

"During the Council I spoke to journalists and the press explaining the ideas about social justice and social order, the right of every man to a decent way of life. I also spoke to them about what the Council could not say. I gave them questions to think about, to find solutions—they are clever people, journalists! . . . . "

The North East of Brazil "a triangle of hunger" is about one fifth of the total area of the country and one third of its population—twenty million in 1960, thirty million today. This is larger than any other nation in Latin America except Argentina, and more densely populated than any other. It is among the largest and most populous underdeveloped areas of the world. There is a humid, fertile coastal strip along the east coast, and a semi-arid interior and north coast. Droughts are frequent, floods too. The rural population is 70% illiterate, unemployed, always in debt to the company stores; the urban population is 60% illiterate, underemployed or unemployed, and rootless. An entrenched farming or sugar plantation oligarchy own almost all the land in huge latifundia, and are fiercely opposed to change. The average annual per capita income is about $120 a year. The best workers leave to try to earn more at low-skill, low-pay jobs in other parts of Brazil. In Recife, more than half the population live in favelas and the infant mortality rate is 60%. Life expectancy in the North-East is about thirty-five years.[14]

15

Amidst cultural terror

"Although for some people it may seem strange, I declare that, in the North-east, Christ is called Jose, Antonio, or Severino. *Ecce Homo!* Here is Christ the Man! Man who needs justice, has the right to justice, deserves justice".[15]

"Severino, son of Severino, nephew of Severino has a bleak life, it is a death in life. He vegetates more than he lives a human life. He does not vegetate like a leafy tree, with its roots filled with life, but like the cactus, his brother. Until today, he has not rebelled. He learned from his illiterate parents and at the church of his lordly landowner boss to be patient, like the Son of God, who has endured so much injustice that he died on the cross to save us".[16]

"Formerly, his employers kept slaves, and they managed to make themselves believe that our brothers were happy in their *senzala,* their slavery. Today, Christian employers manage not to see that this slavery continues, even if not so labelled. The workers have the right to die on the land of their masters. They are given shanties to live in with their wives and children. They have work to do for the boss and, nearly always, permission to cultivate for themselves a small patch of land. The employer conscientiously thinks of himself as a good and generous father in his relations with these labourers. And if it is true that the shanty almost never has water or light or privy, the boss pacifies his mind by thinking that God tempers the wind to the shorn lamb.

"The boss considers it his right to pay whatever he wants to, whenever he wants to, since he is already granting a great favour by providing land and house, giving work, and permitting the labourer to cultivate a small patch of ground.

"And if, tomorrow, the labourer shows ingratitude, pretends

to be a human being, taking an interest in innovations, frequenting radio schools, participating in trade unionism, talking about rights, then the boss is convinced there is cause for alarm: the wind of subversion is blowing—even, who knows, of communism. And then, without the least hesitation or remorse, he sacks the worker, drives him off his lands, and if needs be, demolishes the shanty in which the worker lived with his family".[17]

I finish reading the extract from Dom Helder's first address upon taking possession of the archdiocese of Olinda and Recife on the twelfth of April 1964, as well as extracts from addresses on other occasions. When he joins me I ask him:

"Dom Helder, tell me about your move to Recife?"

He settles himself into the chair beside me, remarking:

"It wasn't easy, in fact it was hard. I had been in Rio for 28 years. It meant leaving many friends and co-workers—but it was God's will. I decided to take none of them with me but to begin afresh . . . .

"I went to Recife only a few days after the Revolution—the military coup—of April 1st. From the beginning I knew I must have the courage to speak the truth, right from the very first moment. At that critical time people spoke of me as the 'Red Archbishop'. They held me responsible for the groups who were calling for reform of the system. They associated me with the attempts President Goulart had made for social change. When the coup—carefully orchestrated by the military—took place, President Goulart fled. The Supreme Military Command took over the country with a General as President. Many of the Catholic Action militants were jailed, so were the leaders of the Rural Unions and MEB under the declared threat of a Communist takeover. Congress members, writers, journalists, media people were also jailed. It was a reign of cultural terror . . . .

"So I had to have the courage to speak out as Archbishop of Recife on the importance of freedom, of justice and of truth in that decisive hour . . . .

"Four days after my Inauguration as bishop we had a meeting of the sixteen bishops of the area to call for social justice in the Northeast, and to appeal for those jailed, the leaders of Catholic Action, of MEB and the Rural Unions whom we supported . . . .

"The next day the Episcopal Palace was raided by soldiers looking for the sister of Miguel Arraes, the deposed Governor of Pernambuco. He too was in prison. I spoke to the General

76

in charge and the troops withdrew, but it was a sign of the times. The military government didn't like progressive bishops . . . .

"In May the Cardinals and Metropolitan Archbishops held a meeting in Rio and issued a statement supporting the new government. They protested their right however to speak out for the poor and oppressed, the victims of injustice . . . .

"In June I had a meeting with the new President, and persuaded him to allow MEB and the Catholic Unions to continue. He too was from the Northeast and we could talk as friends. He often telephoned me to say: 'Let us have a talk together like simple men of Ceara'. He was President for three years, but despite all the private and public appeals anti-Communism continued to be the preoccupation of the Government. Any efforts at reform were seen as Communist-inspired or subversive. A President is often imprisoned by the system".

A Latin American bishop originated the movement that would finally result in the Schema on the Church in the World. Dom Helder Camara . . . . constantly buttonholed visitors to discuss with them the problems of the third world. He kept on repeating: "And now, what are we to do? Are we going to spend all our time debating the internal problems of the Church while two-thirds of mankind is dying of hunger? What have we to say about the problems of underdevelopment? Will the Council express its concern for the great problems of mankind? Are we going to leave Pope John all alone in this great struggle?" In a talk at Domus Mariae (the hostel of Italian Catholic Action occupied by many Italian and Latin American bishops, including Dom Helder) he said, "Is shortage of priests the biggest problem in Latin America? No! It is underdevelopment!" [18]

16

Silenced by law

"On my first visit to Manguinos, the Episcopal Palace in Recife, I threw open all the doors and windows. They have remained open ever since. I wanted everyone of whatever creed to know those doors were always open. Christ came for all men, I always try to remember this. I wanted it to be a place where poor people could be at home, so I had the ornate Bishop's thrones removed. I lived there for four years, until it was possible to make the move to my little house. We now use Manguinos for offices, and all who wish can come there with their problems . . . .

"When I first came to Recife I was away for long periods from the diocese. I had to go to Rome very often as a member of two Commissions, the Lay Apostolate and the mixed Commission working on the document for the Church in the Modern World. The third and fourth sessions of the Council were also held in those years . . . .

"At present I only leave the diocese for very important occasions. I get many invitations to speak abroad about justice and peace. But Pope Paul asked me not to remain longer than 29 days a year away from my diocese, and any request of the Pope is a command for me. The most difficult humiliation for me would be to lose the trust of the Holy Father. I do not mean just Paul VI but any Pope . . . . I am a man of the Church: it's strange . . . . I always need the inner conviction that I am in accord with the Pope".

Here I interject a question:

"Dom Helder, is that why you haven't spoken out about Humanae Vitae or clerical celibacy? People complain that you only speak out about social justice".

Dom Helder replies immediately and very emphatically:

"Because social justice *is* the most important issue, it is at the root of all problems. We have clinics in the diocese where help and advice is given. Priests! I believe we will always need priests with long years of training. But what we need most of all are priests with a thousand reasons for living who would then draw other people to the ministry. We will never have enough priests in Latin America if they have to have long years of training. To respond to the needs of communities we will also have to ordain the Christian leaders in these communities. I will never do this unless Rome approves, but I will try by every means to show that there is no other solution . . . .

"In the meantime I see my role as speaking out about social justice on every occasion, because as a Bishop I have the responsibility to try by every means to change the system in order that the Church be faithful to the Gospel. I would not be worthy of Christ if I remained silent. Every Monday night I have a radio broadcast from Radio Olinda, a simple Gospel message to hundreds of listening groups with twenty participants in each group. The text is chosen and prepared by the groups. The message is usually dramatised and the meaning emphasised for the daily life of the group. I merely contribute a five-minute commentary. When the half-hour programme is over, the listening groups continue for an hour discussing the application of the Gospel message for their daily lives".

Dom Helder pauses and his tone becomes softer.

"Today I am becoming one of the voiceless poor of Brazil. Only on local radio can my voice be heard. The National Press and radio are forbidden to report anything I say. When I am attacked in the most widely read newspapers, I am not allowed the use of the media to reply. If I speak abroad at Press conferences on social justice, condemning the use of torture my words are altered. I am accused of washing Brazil's dirty linen in public. Yet conditions in the North East are steadily getting worse. I must continue to fight for the human rights of my people".

"Everywhere there are men who hunger and thirst for justice. In the poor countries there are men who are ready to fight internal colonialism, in a peaceful but brave and determined way, cost what it may. In the rich countries there are men who are ready to condemn and fight to eradicate the strata of poverty, shameful and flagrant evidence of egoism. In relations between rich and poor countries they are ready to denounce and to fight the injustices of international business practices. Everywhere, in every country, in every community, in every corner of the world, there are Abrahamic minorities who, like Abraham, hope when all hope is gone".[19]

17

Organize for justice

"The atmosphere in the country changed after the coup. Many of the bishops took a stand on law and order and co-operation with the new government. When the CNBB met in Rome during the third session of the Council, I was not re-elected as Secretary General nor as Vice-President of the Conference of Bishops of Latin America. I was to continue in the National Secretariat for Social Action and as regional representative for the 43 bishops of the Northeast, but it was evident that a confrontation between Church and Government was not the will of the majority of the Bishops . . . .

"In Rio I used to think that the Brazilian form of Church-State relationship was an ideal one. Only slowly did I realize that a preoccupation with law and order promoted internal colonialism and that temporal leadership can never be put before our call to be like Christ in denouncing injustice and the legalism of the so-called social order. A relationship between the Church and those in power must be based on this . . . .

"This is not only a Brazilian problem, it is a world-wide problem. It has to be a world-wide struggle for liberation. I believe it will include all the men of good-will of every race and religion who want justice and love and peace . . . . "

Here Dom Helder's voice lifts on a note of hope. There is an invisible straightening of his shoulders.

"I give lectures and speeches all over the world, in the U.S.A., Canada, Europe, Japan—everywhere it is the same—groups of men and women working to build a more just, more human world. I call them the Abrahamic minorities; like Abraham they are ready to sacrifice everything. They work so that poverty can be solved and social justice achieved on an international level . . . .

"I place my hope especially in the groups of young people. They want no part in hypocrisy or discrimination. Sometimes their enthusiasm for causes is condemned. It will be a sad day for our world when youth is no longer confident and enthusiastic . . . .

"When I organized the campaign for 'Action, Justice and Peace' in Brazil—to mobilize the non-violent forces of the world against the violent structures—it was to stimulate these young people to search for an alternative to violence as a solution to world problems".

Dom Helder's face 'comes alive', his eyes gleam as he remembers the movement. As he describes its launching I can see the groups of young actors, hear their songs and the refrain sung by the large audience, the clapping of hands, the Brazilian beat and rhythm of the music set to the words of non-violent revolution. The meaning of those words, the theme of the revolutionary love of God for all mankind motivates Dom Helder's life and work . . . .

I remember another account told to me about a suggestion of Dom Helder's that the people of Recife should hold a Christmas festival, a sort of medieval production in which everyone would take part. Each group of people wrote and enacted their own part of the drama, the technocrats, the engineers, the school-girls, the University students, the workers, the peasants, even the 'victims of prostitution'. It was held in the huge football stadium which was jammed with hundreds of people, and the Governor of Pernambuco did not dare stop the performance because there were so many people involved. Imagine the scene as the 'victims of prostitution' came on stage and the throbbing Brazilian music told their story:

VICTIMS OF PROSTITUTION
MUSIC: *My story*—(Chico Buarte de Hollanda)

> And you, who in your face bear
> the sleep of sleepless nights
> the anguish of lost hopes,
> You who drag
> the weight of frustration and weariness
> from being so much used and never loved.
> You who are the victims of a society
> that bred umemployment and hunger,
> that led you to exchange body for bread,

that extracts pleasure from you and refuses you a name
that hides you that it may exploit you,
and keeps you beyond the pale.
You, white slaves, women of the so-called easy life,
who carry the burden of the blackest slavery.
You, who live in the forbidden streets,
so often visited and trodden.
You, who are looked upon as lost women,
albeit so sought after and never found.
You, who guard in your heart,
And reveal to those who have eyes to see,
the flame and the ardour,
the dedication and the love,
the simplicity and the candour,
the willingness and gentleness,
of Magdalene.
You, all of you victims of prostitution, what are you hungry
and thirsty for?

What are we hungry and thirsty for?
A thirst to love greatly and be loved,
A hunger to be someone, to be accepted,
rather than, like an object, coveted.
To have the rich blessing of a home,
and of a husband's companionship,
to bring up sons and daughters.
To meet people who receive us without humiliating,
who understand us without condemning,
To have the chance
to develop our talents,
our gifts, our feelings.
And how they treat us,
so many maladjusted men! . . . .
Let them cease their beatings,
we too are flesh and bone.
We deserve better treatment,
And in the health clinics, what treatment we receive!

As our right, in the name of justice, we want to be
understood.
Stop the humiliations. We are people, we are life!
At least among Christians
let there be a place for us.

Let them extend a hand
Let them not repeat the sin of the self-righteous Pharisees.
Let them be a sign of Christ
    for this is what they're in the world for,
    to be the signs of forgiveness!

"We are all convinced that freedom is a divine gift which must be preserved at any price. Let us liberate, in the fullest sense of the word, every human creature in our midst".[20]

18

Arrest me

This morning a friend of Dom Helder's speaks of a recent incident where a co-worker of Dom Helder's disappeared without trace.

"The neighbours insisted that the police had taken him away. The police denied any knowledge of the event. Such disappearances are common in Brazil. Dom Helder was quick to act. He packed his little bag and went to the police station.

'Here I am! Please arrest me but let my friend go. He has a wife and family. I know why he was arrested. I am happy to take his place'.

'No! No! Monseignor! We never heard of this man. Why should we arrest you? There is some misunderstanding.'" . . . .

I ask Dom Helder about the incident and his face becomes suddenly serious. His eyes are full of pain as he answers:

"It is very, very difficult. It is most difficult for me because they are arrested on my account, because they associate with me on projects and work for social justice. One of my closest friends Pe. Antonio Henrique Neto who worked with the students at the University was beaten, shot in the head and then hanged".

Dom Helder rises and goes into the study. He returns with a book, sits down, opens it, and passes me a folded card. On one side is a photo of the disfigured Pe. Neto. I can't find any words. Dom Helder begins to speak again.

"The day of his funeral all the traffic in Recife was halted. Crowds came from miles around. They all carried white handkerchiefs and waved them in farewell to the young priest . . . . "

Here Dom Helder's voice breaks and he cannot continue. It is the only time I am to see him break down . . . .

This incredibly courageous little man is overcome at the remembrance of the suffering inflicted on his friend. He understands well the reason for the brutal murder, the harassing of other co-workers, the machine-gunning of his house, the threatening phone calls. He has never moved from his position to defend human rights, to denounce injustice, to be part of the struggle to eliminate oppressive structures of any kind, but the risk to others' lives is a consideration he cannot ignore and it must necessarily curtail his activities.

Dom Helder continues in a quiet voice:

"The only violence I can understand is the violence of a peace maker, the non-violence of Christ, of Gandhi or of Martin Luther King. . . .

Injustice always breeds violence. The violent reaction to injustice spawns further violence in its turn. Many young people are driven to this violent reaction because of the inaction of Church or State. I can understand them, Che Guevara or Camilo Torres — they tire of non-violent efforts and resort to revolution. But the only answer lies in non-violent pressure . . . .

"In Latin America the military forces can easily, certainly ultimately crush violent action for liberation. But most of all the majority of the people, the masses are not ready for the struggle. They have to be encouraged to struggle for life. They certainly do not have the courage to die. First they must be made more aware of their dignity as human beings, as children of God before whom all men are equal. Then they will be ready for the struggle for a great non-violent action for justice and peace.

"I see no dichotomy between soul and body. A man is a single undivided unit; we can't separate his 'religious part' from the rest of him".

Dom Helder raises his arm and his voice and declaims:

"Je ne suis pas pasteur d'ames, je suis pasteur d'hommes?"

"Man must be dealt with by both Church and State as a unit, his rights respected, his opinions listened to, his co-operation in the task of world transformation requested and acknowledged. God did not give us only the care of souls. Formerly one said: in my diocese of Recife there are 1,200,000 souls. No! It is true that there are 1,200,000 souls but they are incarnate souls. I cannot make this distinction, this separation between body and soul".

How happy are the poor in spirit;
theirs is the kingdom of heaven.
Happy the gentle:
they shall have the earth for their heritage.
Happy those who mourn:
they shall be comforted.
Happy those who hunger and thirst for what is right:
they shall be satisfied.
Happy the merciful:
they shall have mercy shown them.
Happy the pure in heart:
they shall see God.
Happy the peacemakers:
they shall be called sons of God.
Happy those who are persecuted in the cause of right:
theirs is the kingdom of heaven.[21]

19

Final testimony

As I see the people cluster about Dom Helder everywhere we go I am reminded of another pilgrim—Jesus Christ with the people of Galilee. Many of those I speak with illustrate this point. They do not want their identity to be disclosed for security reasons, but the essence of Dom Helder's spirit runs through their tapes.

"On the 5 August 1973 there was a big festival for the installation of the newly-appointed Archbishop of Fortaleza in Ceara , the very poor state of the North-east where Dom Helder himself was born. Thirty-eight bishops and archbishops and two cardinals came to the ceremony and Dom Helder was among them . . . .

"Of course everybody who was somebody in the city and everybody whom they say was nobody, but of course really important, was present. They all came to the Cathedral for the ceremony and I was there representing the Council. I was sitting behind the General in charge of the military in Fortaleza and next to him was the Naval Commandant. All the bishops were behind the altar, because there were too many there to walk in the procession. Only the archbishops and the cardinals came in with the new bishops, and the Master of Ceremonies announced the names of the archbishops and their cities as they came in. The last one mentioned was Dom Helder Camara of Recife. Well! the whole Cathedral burst into applause. It was something quite spontaneous, and I saw the General just in front of me jump in his seat! I was as happy as can be! . . . . The General and the Naval Officer just could not believe their eyes. They even stood up to see if it was really true, this applause that was bursting out all over the place.

"Well, the ceremony went on, and after it they all went out in procession, the archbishops and the bishops preceding the new archbishop. Several times the procession halted because people came to try and kiss Dom Helder's hands or his garments, or to try to touch him. It was really the most moving sight, and the strange thing was that Dom Helder wanted to hide himself—he is already a small man and he was trying to make himself as small as possible! But his charisma is so strong that it transcends everything . . . .

"Even while he was sitting at the altar when they were all celebrating, Dom Helder hardly moved—he just tried to be as small as possible. Everybody was looking at him all the time, and people acted as though they had seen Christ himself; I think that people can't go wrong if they feel this charisma in Dom Helder. They feel the spirit of God there and they know they have somebody who really loves the poor, and who lives like one of them . . . .

"Some people think he is a communist, a crazy man, a demagogue, while many others would agree with what I think— that he's a man full of the Spirit of God; a prophet of the Third World. A prophet is always a person who is a nuisance to other people, because he brings them face to face with themselves. He puts a mirror in front of their faces and they don't like what they see and that's why they get so angry".

"You know we have paid assassins in the North-east, and there was somebody who hated Dom Helder, and paid a man to kill him. Well, this man went to the poor little house where he lives and knocked, and as usual Dom Helder came himself to open the door. The man said:
'I want to speak to Dom Helder'.
'I am Dom Helder'.
The man was astonished.
'You are Dom Helder?'
'Yes, what do you want? Come in'.
'He took the man in, gave him a chair and said:
'Do you need me for anything? What do you want?'
'No, no, I don't want to have anything to do with you because you are not one of those that you kill'.
'Kill? Why do you want to kill?'
'Because I was paid to kill you, but I can't kill you'.
'If you are paid, why don't you kill me? I will go to the Lord';
but the man said:
'No, you are one of the Lord's' and he left and went away . . .

This is typical of Dom Helder. He has no fear of anyone because his life is not his. His life belongs to Jesus, even if he has fear what worse can you do to a person except take his life? Even if you torture him . . . . ''

"I feel he is getting more and more detached from earthly things; at the same time that he gets more and more immersed in earthly things. I think it's really what the Lord said, that you have to be in the world, but not of the world. That's exactly what he is. Nothing can stop him because he has given up his life for God . . . . ''

"One day, in 1970, we were working at the Bishop's Conference in Brasilia, and Dom Helder came just for a few moments at the height of the persecution against him, and I asked him:
'Dom Helder, how are you?'
He said,
'Well, I'm not important. I'm well . . . I'm not important . . . It's those around me'.
Then he said:
'They are trying to prune all the branches . . . . '
He meant the persecution of those who collaborated with him in his work, and that, to him, was much worse than if they had made an attempt on his own life . . . .
For me, that is Dom Helder . . . . He is really the witness of Christ to the Church, not only in Brazil, but in the whole of the World''.

NOTES AND SOURCES

Note No.

p. 8   1.   de Broucker, J. *The Violence of a Peacemaker:* Orbis Books, 1969.

         2.   Ibid.

p. 26   3.   Leonard, P. J. *Dom Helder Camara,* D.Phil. dissertation, St. Louis University, Missouri, U.S.A. 1974.

p. 34   4.   Ibid.

p. 40   5.   Ibid.

p. 46   6.   Bruneau, T. C. *The Political Transformation of the Brazilian Catholic Church,* Cambridge University Press, 1974.

p. 50   7.   Statement in which Dom Helder collaborated.

p. 54   8.   Statement in which Dom Helder collaborated.

p. 58   9.   Dom Helder Camara.

p. 61   10.   Dom Helder Camara.

p. 61   11.   President Juscelino Kubitschck.

p. 66   12.   Dom Helder Camara.

p. 70   13.   Fesquet, H. quoted in P. J. Leonard, op. cit.

p. 74   14.   Centro de Estatistica Religosa e Investigaçoes Sociais, Rio de Janeiro.

p. 75   15.   Address of Dom Helder on arrival in Recife as Archbishop, April 12, 1964.

p. 75   16.   Address of Dom Helder at the School of Polytechnics, Campina Grande, December 17, 1966.

p. 76   17.   Address of Dom Helder at the School of Law of the Federal University of Rio Grande de Norte in Natal, December 8, 1966.

p. 78   18.   Leonard, P. J. op. cit.

p. 82   19.   Weigner, Gladys V Bereshard Moosbruger: *La Voix du Monde sans Voix:* Action de Carêmê des Catholiques, Zurich 1971.

p. 88   20.   Inaugural speech of Dom Helder Camara on taking possession of the See of Recife. April 12, 1964.

p. 92   21.   The Sermon on the Mount, Matthew 5: 1-10, Jerusalem Bible.